If you were a

Verb

by Michael Dahl

illustrated by Sara Gray

PICTURE WINDOW BOOKS
Minneapolis, Minnesota

verb (vor vb) a word that is used to express an action or condition

Editor: Christianne Jones
Designer: Nathan Gassman
Page Production: Tracy Kaehler
Creative Director: Keith Griffin
Editorial Director: Carol Jones
The illustrations in this book
were created with acrylics.

Picture Window Books
5115 Excelsior Boulevard
Suite 232
Minneapolis, MN 55416
877-845-8392
www.picturewindowbooks.com

Looking for verbs?
Watch for the big, colorful words in the example sentences.

Special thanks to our advisers for their expertise:

Rosemary G. Palmer, Ph.D., Department of Literacy
College of Education, Boise State University

Susan Kesselring, M.A., Literacy Educator
Rosemount—Apple Valley—Eagan (Minnesota) School District

Library of Congress Cataloging-in-Publication Data
Dahl, Michael.
If you were a verb / by Michael Dahl ; illustrated by Sara Gray.
p. cm. — (Word fun)
ISBN 1-4048-1354-3 (hardcover)
1. English language—Verb—Juvenile literature. I. Gray, Sara, ill.
II. Title. III. Series.

PE1271.D34 2006   2005021855
428.1—dc22

If you were a verb ...

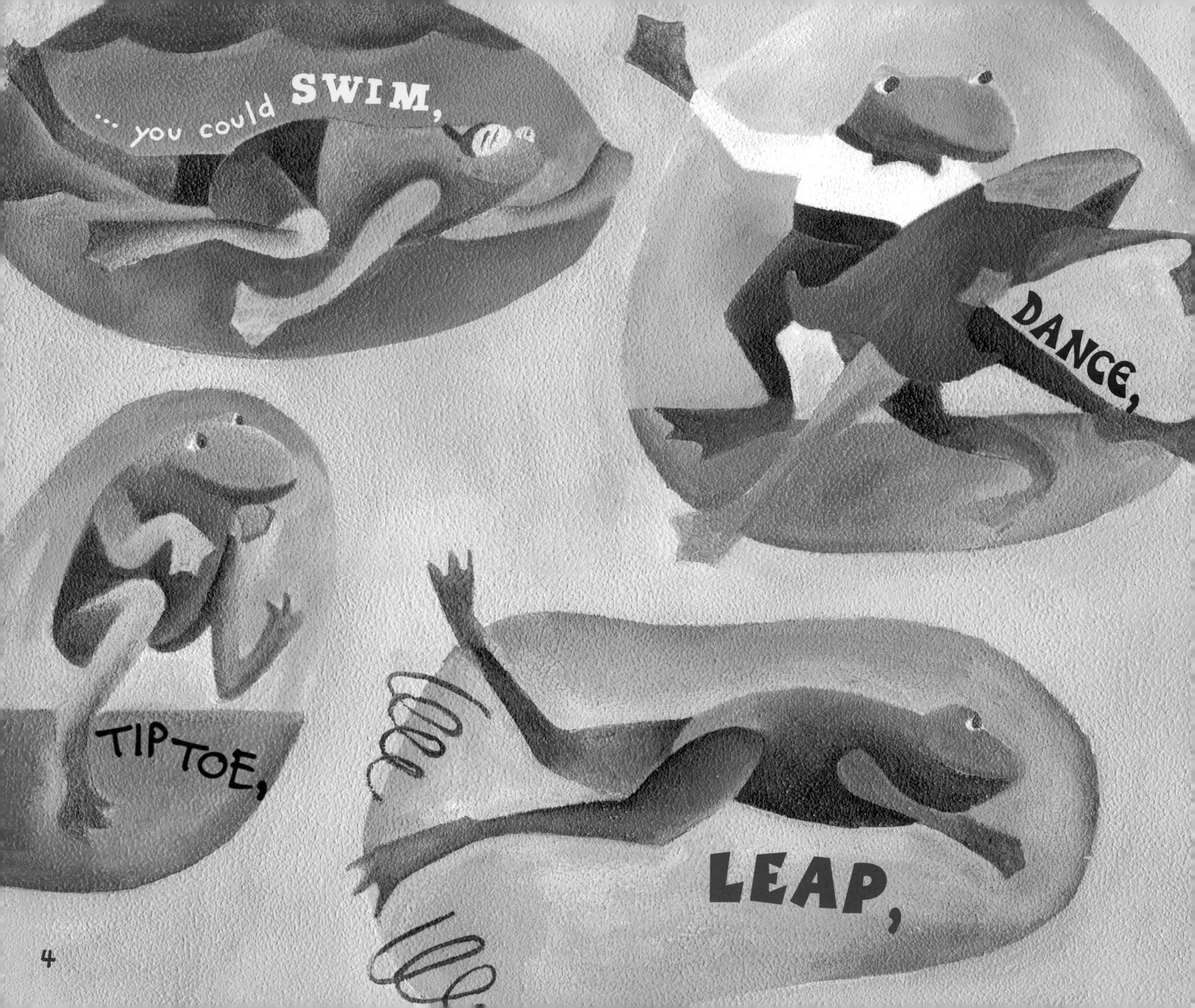

... you could SWIM,

DANCE,

TIPTOE,

LEAP,

PADDLE,

CARTWHEEL,

TRAVEL,

or PLUNGE.

Verbs get things going!

If you were a verb, you could BALANCE and BEND, TWIST and TURN,

6

SWOOP and SOAR.

If you were a verb, you would appear in every sentence.

You would be in every book, every newspaper, every magazine, and every letter ever written.

8

9

If you were a verb,
you could be an action.

The mighty ship SAILS out of the harbor.

Waves **CRASH** against its side.
Seagulls **SCREAM** overhead.

If you were a verb, extra words would help you show action. These extra words are called helping verbs.

You **MAY** give the usher your ticket now.

The popcorn **WILL BE** popping soon.

The movie *HAS* started on the big screen.

If you were a helping verb, you would have 23 members in your family: may, might, must, be, being, been, am, are, is, was, were, do, does, did, should, could, would, have, had, has, will, can, shall.

If you were a verb, you could link things together. You would be a linking verb. Sometimes linking verbs are called state-of-being verbs.

The swimmer **WAS** tired.

The beach ball **IS** floating.

The lifeguards **WERE** done for the day.

If you were a linking verb, your most common forms would be is, am, were, was, are, be, being, and been.

If you were a verb, you would change when time passed. You could be in past tense, present tense, or future tense.

Last night, the bicycles GLIDED through the park.

Now, the bicycles **GLIDE** through the park.

Tomorrow, the bicycles **WILL GLIDE** through the park.

If you were a verb, you would change when the number of people or things change.

One acrobat SWINGS above the crowd,

but five acrobats *SWING* above the crowd.

If you were a verb, you would get together with other verbs to make cool and exciting sentences.

The rocket SPEEDS toward the space station

that **WHIRLS** and **SPINS** above Earth.

You could always be moving ...

... if you were a **verb!**

FUN with VERBS

Verbs can be full of action. Verbs can also be quiet.

Directions: Think of an action verb, such as running, jumping, or flying. Then make your friends guess what the verb is by acting it out. See how quickly they can figure out what your secret verb is. Take turns acting out action verbs and guessing.

Next, choose a quiet verb, such as standing, sleeping, thinking, staring, wishing, or hiding. Take turns acting out quiet verbs and guessing.

Is it harder to act out an action verb or a quiet verb?

Fact: If you look up a verb in the dictionary, you will see the abbreviation "v" or "vb" next to it. The "v" or "vb" stands for verb.

23

Glossary

acrobat—a person who performs stunts

glide—to move without any effort

harbor—a sheltered place along the coast
   where ships and boats anchor

soar—to fly high in the air

swoop—to go down suddenly

tiptoe—to walk quietly

usher—a person who leads people to their seats

To Learn More

At the Library

Cleary, Brian P. *To Root, to Toot, to Parachute: What Is a
   Verb?* Minneapolis, Minn.: Carolrhoda Books, 2001.

Heller, Ruth. *Kites Sail High: A Book About Verbs.* New York:
   Grosset & Dunlap, 1988.

Schneider, R. M. *Add It, Dip It, Fix It: A Book of Verbs.*
   Boston: Houghton Mifflin, 1995.

On the Web

FactHound offers a safe, fun way to find Internet
sites related to this book. All of the sites on
FactHound have been researched by our staff.

1. Visit *www.facthound.com*
2. Type in this special
   code for age-appropriate
   sites: 1404813543
3. Click on the FETCH IT button.

Your trusty FactHound will fetch the best sites for you!

Look for all of the books
in the Word Fun series:

If You Were a Noun
1-4048-1355-1

If You Were a Verb
1-4048-1354-3

If You Were an Adjective
1-4048-1356-X

If You Were an Adverb
1-4048-1357-8